Milliontality

Austyn Ingram

Published by Austyn Ingram, 2022.

Milliontality

Austyn ingram

Published by Austyn ingram, 2024.

MILLIONTALITY

First edition. November 23, 2024.

Copyright © 2024 Austyn ingram.

ISBN: 979-8215906910

Written by Austyn ingram.

Introduction

Chapter 1: the fundamentals of law of attraction

Chapter 2: how to use the law of attraction to

Chapter 3: how the law of attraction can improve

Y<u>our life</u>

<u>Positive thoughts can attract positive experiences</u>

austyn ingram

<u>When you think of something positive, you invite</u>
<u>It to your life</u>
<u>Concentration makes everything powerful</u>
<u>Trust your emotions rather than overthinking</u>
<u>Accelerate the power of manifestation through concentration</u>
<u>Imagine things the way you want them to be to</u>
<u>See the changes</u>

powerfulpositivethinkingcanattractmore

<u>Positive things</u>
<u>Keep in mind that you can be successful</u>
<u>Don't be depressed because of your failure</u>
<u>Stay away from shows that encourage negative</u>
<u>Thoughts</u>
<u>Understand that you are the architect of your life</u>
<u>And relationships</u>

<u>Use your dreams as a guide</u>

Chapter 4: the science behind the law of attraction

Chapter 5: how the power of visualization can help achieve your goals

Chapter 6: the mindset of a successful person

Make sure to always take the first step and "start"

Your tasks

Always strive for continuous improvement

Develop confidence in your own skills

Accept who you are

Chapter 7: daily lifestyle habits of a successful person

Introduction

You've probably heard of the Law of Attraction, but you're not sure what it is or how to put it to use in your life. The Law of Attraction is a concept of harmonious alignment that allows you to attract the things you want into your life. It is a concept that has been around for thousands of years. Whatever it is that you desire, the Law of Attraction can assist you in obtaining it. You may be already familiar with the concept of law. The Law of Attraction has become increasingly popular in recent years, thanks to the work of authors such as Esther and Jerry Hicks, Michael Losier, and others, as well as the mega-hit The Secret by Rhonda Byrne, which has brought the principles of this universal spiritual law to a wider audience.

The Law of Attraction ensures that whatever you most desire and think about most frequently will manifest in your life. You are free to eat whatever you want. You might be interested in:

- Longevity or good health are important factors in life.

- Some of life's finer things, such as a sleek automobile or a lovely piece of jewelry, are a luxury.

- This person would make an excellent romantic partner.

- A well-paying job or a stepping stone to a new profession

- Spiritual growth and development

- Happiness and tranquility of mind

4

Each one of those objectives is perfectly reasonable and attainable.

The universal Law of Attraction is constantly at work, bringing about the experiences, relationships, and things that you desire the most in your life. If you are concerned about breaking a bone, you will most likely draw it in, which will result in the break occurring. Fear attracts more of the thing you are afraid of and vice versa.

But don't lose heart! The good news is that the same is also true in the other direction. When you have a strong desire to manifest money, your desire, when combined with feelings of excited anticipation, can bring you financial success. Your thoughts can be shifted to create more positive and happy experiences in your life, and transformational thinking has the potential to completely transform your life. It doesn't stop there, either. When you work in harmony with the Law of Attraction and with other like-minded individuals, you have the potential to make a positive difference in the world. Through the power of your heart and mind, you and everyone who is consciously working with the Law of Attraction become co-creators with the Divine, which is a powerful experience.

These are not difficult procedures to learn and master. As you begin to work with the Law of Attraction, you can use this book to become informed, inspired, and confident in your efforts. Thanks to the more than 50 exercises that are simple to implement, you'll be well on your way to engaging in transformational thinking, which will bring about exciting and positive changes in your life!

Chapter 1: The Fundamentals Of Law Of Attraction

The law of attraction is undoubtedly the most well-known of the twelve universal laws because it receives the most media attention. Put another way, this spiritual principle proposes that what attracts like and that positive thinking can usher in a more positive reality.

In this article, you'll learn how to understand the law of attraction, how it differs from other forms of magic, and how you can use it to achieve your goals.

What Is The Law Of Attraction And How Does It Work?

"Watch your thoughts, for they become your words; watch your words, for they become your actions; watch your actions, for they become your habits; watch your habits, for they become your character; watch your character, for it becomes your destiny," said Lao Tzu, an ancient Chinese philosopher.

According to historical evidence, the concept of attracting what we put out has been around for a long time. Many believe that Buddha was the one who first introduced it to the world.

The law of attraction operates based on the three principles outlined below:

"Like Attracts Like"

is rooted in the belief that similar energies attract one another, a principle that spans various fields, including psychology, philosophy, and metaphysics. This idea suggests that the energies we emit—our thoughts, emotions, and actions—tend to resonate with and attract similar frequencies, influencing our personal relationships, career pathways, and overall experiences in life.

At its core, "Like Attracts Like" embodies the Law of Attraction, which posits that positive or negative thoughts bring positive or negative experiences into a person's life. This principle emphasizes the power of mindset; when individuals focus on positive outcomes, resilience, and abundance, they tend to create opportunities that align with these optimistic perspectives. Conversely, dwelling on negativity or fear can manifest further negativity, leading to a cycle of undesirable outcomes. This is evident in many people's experiences: those who foster a positive outlook often find themselves surrounded by supportive and uplifting individuals, while negativity can lead to isolation or toxic relationships.

In interpersonal relationships, "Like Attracts Like" can be observed quite prominently. People often gravitate towards others who share similar values, interests, and beliefs. This phenomenon explains why friendships and partnerships frequently form between individuals with common life experiences or perspectives. For example, communities often flourish where people share a common passion or goal, creating supportive environments that nurture growth and collaboration. In professional settings, coworkers with aligned visions and work ethics can foster a synergistic atmosphere that propels collective achievements.

The relevance of "Like Attracts Like" extends into personal growth and self-improvement. When individuals work towards self-betterment—whether through education, self-reflection, or emotional healing—they often encounter a significant shift in their social circles. As one evolves, they may find that old relationships begin to fade, while new, more compatible connections emerge. This transformation reflects the idea that as one raises their vibrational frequency, they attract those who resonate at similar levels, creating deeper, more meaningful connections.

The concept is also echoed in the realm of business and entrepreneurship. Successful entrepreneurs frequently emphasize the importance of surrounding oneself with like-minded individuals who share similar aspirations and ambitions. By collaborating with others who boast a mutual drive and vision, they can amplify their success and inspire innovative solutions. This symbiotic relationship illustrates the practical application of "Like Attracts Like," showcasing how aligned goals can enhance productivity and satisfaction.

Furthermore, the psychological implications of this principle can be analyzed through the lens of cognitive dissonance. People naturally seek consistency between their beliefs and actions—when there is a discrepancy, it often leads to discomfort. Consequently, individuals may form connections or pursue pursuits that align with their existing beliefs to maintain a sense of harmony. This psychological drive further reinforces the idea that attraction is not purely surface-level; it delves into the fundamental need for congruence in our lives.

In conclusion, "Like Attracts Like" is a multifaceted principle that illustrates how our energies, thoughts, and emotions influence our experiences and relationships. By harnessing this concept, individuals can focus on cultivating a positive mindset and nurturing connections that serve their highest good. Ultimately, acknowledging and embracing the law of attraction can lead to personal empowerment, deeper relationships, and a more fulfilling life. Encouraging self-awareness and intentionality in our thoughts and relationships can pave the way for a life steeped in alignment and positivity, illustrating the profound truth behind the idea that like truly does attract like.

Nature Abhors Vacuum

As a result of this principle, it is suggested that empty space cannot truly exist and must always be filled by something else. As a result, it's critical to clear the way for positive change in your life by getting rid of all clutter.

Like decluttering your desk or bedroom, decluttering your mind is necessary to have more room to attract new things that are more beneficial to your life.

Remember That The Present Is Ideal

The third and final aspect of the law of attraction is the perfection of the present moment, which is the final step in the process.

If we look for it, there will always be unhappiness about it; however, finding ways to make things better, rather than dwelling on what is wrong, is essential to shifting your reality into one that attracts what you want to be happy about.

That is not to say that you cannot acknowledge negativity or experience negative emotions due to it. Then we're getting into the territory of spiritual bypassing or toxic positivity. As an alternative, it is important to focus on doing what you can right now to improve any negative situation while allowing the rest to fall into place.

What the law of attraction is "not"

Of course, positive thinking and belief in one's own abilities will not bring one's dreams to fruition. You, too, must put in the necessary effort!

This entails living by your objectives and taking the steps necessary to bring them to fruition, among other things.

Even if your goal is to run a marathon in less than four hours, you will still need to receive the necessary training and treat your body with respect during those weeks and months leading up to the race. Starting from there, layering on some positive mantras and visualizations can help you further cement your intention with the universe.

It's important for anyone prone to worry about understanding that the law of attraction is not a punishment. As Kaiser points out, "When people first learn about and begin to practice this law, they may be concerned that if they have negative thoughts or low vibrations, Low vibrations can also have a significant impact on our physical, emotional, and mental wellbeing. Low vibrations are often associated with negative emotions such as fear, anxiety, guilt, shame, and anger. When we are experiencing low vibrations, it can feel like we are stuck in a negative cycle that is difficult to break.

One of the ways that low vibrations can affect us is by impacting our energy levels. When we are experiencing low vibrations, it can feel like our energy is drained, leaving us feeling tired and sluggish. This can make it difficult to stay motivated and productive, leading to a sense of apathy and disengagement.

Low vibrations can also impact our emotional wellbeing. When we are experiencing low vibrations, we may feel stuck in negative emotions such as sadness, hopelessness, and despair. This can impact our mood and outlook, leading to a sense of negativity and pessimism.

Another way that low vibrations can affect us is by impacting our relationships with others. When we are experiencing low vibrations, we may be more irritable, withdrawn, and less interested in connecting with others. This can lead to a sense of isolation and disconnection, making it difficult to build and maintain healthy relationships.

One of the challenges with low vibrations is that they can be self-perpetuating. When we are stuck in a cycle of negative emotions and low vibrations, it can be difficult to break free. This can lead to a sense of helplessness and hopelessness, making it difficult to take positive action or make meaningful changes in our lives.

It's important to recognize when we are experiencing low vibrations and take steps to address them. This may involve practices such as mindfulness, meditation, or exercise, which can help to elevate our mood and energy levels. It may also involve seeking support from friends or professional help, such as therapy or counseling.

Overall, low vibrations can have a significant impact on our physical, emotional, and social wellbeing. By recognizing and addressing low vibrations, we can take steps to improve our overall health and wellbeing, leading to a more positive and fulfilling life.

With this they will be able to cause harm to themselves or others." There are no such things as "perfect people," and when we are going through a difficult time, we can use the law as "a mirror of our own mindset and self-worth."

In addition, keep in mind that, at a certain point in the manifestation process, "it's critical to surrender and allow the Universe to take the wheel," as Richardson says. Opportunities, people, and resources can appear out of nowhere, so keep an open mind to what may come your way. Things may not turn out the way you had hoped (in fact, they most likely will not), and that's perfectly fine.

Chapter 2: how to use the law of

Attraction to achieve your dreams

You've probably heard of the law of attraction or books like The Secret, even if you've never tried your hand at working with universal laws. The law of attraction (as well as many other universal laws) is a natural law that states that like attracts like and that opposites attract.

Almost everything on our planet (and in the universe) is made up of energy and vibrates constantly. Lastly, the law of attraction states that everyone attracts what they put out into the universe through the use of energy and vibration they emit.

Although most humanity is aware of universal laws such as the law of attraction, they either never learn about them or choose not to believe in them. However, there is some good news:

Regardless of your religious beliefs, you are constantly acting as a human magnet, sending out vibrational frequencies to the universe and receiving the same energy back. There's no way around using the law of attraction to your advantage. You're doing it regularly.

The law of attraction is constantly in operation. It makes no difference whether you believe in it or not. It's the same as saying you don't believe in the law of attraction and that you don't believe in the force of gravity at the same time. It makes no difference to the universe whether you believe in it or not.

Of course, you can choose not to believe in it and continue to work your asses off for the rest of your life, wondering why you aren't getting what you desire. However, I'm here to tell you that you don't have to work 80 hours a week to live a fulfilling life. Furthermore, I'm here to encourage you to believe that it is possible to live a joyful life filled with ease while also obtaining everything you desire.

Was there a time when you thought about a friend with whom you hadn't spoken in a long time, and then later in the day you heard from them?

Isn't that crazy?

It's common knowledge that when things like this happen, it's just a coincidence. It is not the case. It's a phenomenon known as the law of attraction. So, if this device is effective, why isn't it being used by everyone?

The reason is that 99 percent of the population is completely incorrect.

When it comes to the law of attraction, the following is what the majority of people believe:

"If I think of a million dollars and concentrate on it for a long time, the universe will send it to me."

Guess what? It turns out to be true. That is not the way things work.

As an example, here's what it looks like in practice:

Suppose you concentrate your efforts on becoming a millionaire, believe that it is what you deserve, and get your asses up and actually put in the effort. In that case, the universe will assist you in finding ways to make it happen.

You see the difference, don't you? Good.

However, the law of attraction is not solely based on your thoughts; a significant portion of it is based on your actions. You won't be able to manifest anything unless you get your ass up and do something.

It's not just about what you think and believe; it's about the combination of believing in the right thing, trusting in the universe, and taking massive, determined action that makes the difference.

The majority of people try to avoid being noticed. Instead of sharing our values, wishes, and dreams with the world, we choose to keep them to ourselves instead. And, while some may refer to this as being introverted, most of us are simply afraid to admit what we really want. We are so afraid of failing to achieve our objectives that we have decided not to discuss them at all.

I even know people who are afraid of getting what they want because they are unsure if they will deal with the consequences. And guess what happens if you aren't certain about what you want in life: nothing happens. You're not going to get it.

Steps To Implementing The Law Of Attraction In Your Life

The people who are skilled at raising their vibration and maintaining it for the majority of their time are considered manifestation pros. To be positive and cheerful all of the time is obviously impossible, but that is not what you need at this time. It's simply a matter of letting go of unneeded negativity and bad vibes and putting your attention on the life you want to live.

The entire manifestation process is based on our dominant feelings and beliefs at the time of manifestation. As a result, our superior thoughts and, more importantly, the feelings that accompany these thoughts cause manifestation. As a result, it is these feelings that we want to pay attention to in our daily lives.

1. Listed below are simple steps you can take to raise your vibration, increase your energy, and attract the greatness you've always desired: Set clear intentions: Begin by setting clear intentions for what you want to manifest in your life. Be specific and focus on what you want, rather than what you don't want. Write down your intentions and visualize them as if they have already come true.

2. Believe in what you want: Belief is a powerful force that can help you manifest your desires. Trust that the universe will bring you what you want and focus on positive outcomes.

3. Practice gratitude: Cultivate a sense of gratitude for what you already have in your life. This can help to shift your focus away from lack and scarcity and towards abundance and positivity.

4. Visualize your success: Spend time each day visualizing yourself achieving your goals and living the life you desire. Use your imagination to create a clear picture in your mind of what you want to manifest.

5. Take inspired action: While the Law of Attraction is powerful, it is important to take action towards your goals. This means taking steps that align with your intentions and moving towards what you want to manifest.
6. Release resistance: Let go of any resistance or negative beliefs that may be holding you back from manifesting your desires. Release any doubts or fears and trust in the process.
7. Practice self-care: Take care of yourself and your wellbeing. This means getting enough rest, eating well, and taking time for activities that bring you joy and fulfillment.

Implementing the Law of Attraction in your life requires commitment, consistency, and a willingness to believe in the power of the universe to bring you what you want. By following these steps, you can begin to manifest positive changes and live the life you desire.

Meditation is a powerful practice that can help individuals get into a positive frequency, fostering emotional well-being and mental clarity. By focusing and calming the mind, meditation cultivates a state of awareness that enhances positivity and reduces stress.

First, meditation promotes relaxation by encouraging deep breathing and mindful awareness. When we meditate, we shift our focus away from the chaotic thoughts and distractions of daily life, allowing our bodies to enter a state of rest. This deep relaxation helps lower cortisol levels, which is the stress hormone, leading to a more peaceful and positive mindset.

Moreover, meditation encourages self-reflection, allowing individuals to connect with their inner selves. Through regular practice, one can develop greater self-awareness and empathy, improving emotional intelligence. As individuals recognize and acknowledge their thoughts and feelings, they are better equipped to challenge negative thought patterns and replace them with positive affirmations.

Visualization techniques in meditation can also enhance positivity. By visualizing desired outcomes, individuals can create a mental image of success, joy, or inner peace. This practice aligns their energy with their aspirations, allowing them to attract positive experiences and opportunities into their lives.

Additionally, mindfulness meditation cultivates an attitude of gratitude, which is essential for achieving a positive frequency. By focusing on the present moment, individuals can appreciate the simple joys and beauty in their lives, fostering a sense of contentment and fulfillment.

Incorporating meditation into daily routines can yield profound benefits, including reduced anxiety, improved focus, and heightened resilience. Even a few minutes of meditation each day can create a ripple effect, shifting one's overall mindset toward positivity. Thus, meditation serves as a valuable tool for individuals seeking to elevate their emotional frequency and enhance their life's quality.

Be Involved In Activities That You Enjoy

When we are engaged in activities that we enjoy, our frequency automatically rises. You can instantly change your mood, raise your vibration, and attract even more of what you enjoy by eating food you enjoy, meeting people you love, visiting places that light up your soul, or participating in activities that make you happy.

Far too often, we believe that we must strive for happiness and become so focused on our objectives that we lose sight of the importance of enjoying our lives. However, by demonstrating to the universe that you appreciate your days, you will attract even more happiness and ease into your life.

Have A Gratitude Journal

One of the most effective ways to raise your vibration and use the law of attraction is to express gratitude for what you already have. And it's incredibly simple.

Simply put, a gratitude journal is a place where you can record everything you're thankful for, including your home, the people you're surrounded by, your health (including access to food, water, and education), and other blessings.

1. Once you decide to practice gratitude, you'll discover that you already have a plethora of things to be grateful for. Choose a journal: Choose a journal that you enjoy writing in and that inspires you. It could be a simple notebook, a fancy journal, or an app on your phone or computer.

2. Set aside time: Set aside a few minutes each day to write in your gratitude journal. You might choose to do this in the morning, before bed, or at another time that works for you.

3. Start small: Begin by writing down just a few things you're grateful for each day. This could include simple things like a good cup of coffee, a kind word from a friend, or a beautiful sunset.

4. Be specific: As you get more comfortable with your gratitude practice, try to be more specific about what you're grateful for. For example, instead of just writing "my job," you might write "I'm grateful for my job because it allows me to support my family and pursue my passions."

5. Focus on the positive: When writing in your gratitude journal, focus on the positive aspects of your life. Try to avoid dwelling on negative thoughts or experiences.

6. Be consistent: Consistency is key when it comes to gratitude journaling. Make it a daily habit to write down at least a few things you're grateful for each day.

7. Reflect on your progress: Over time, take some time to reflect on how your gratitude practice is affecting your life. Are you feeling more positive and optimistic? Are you noticing more abundance and opportunities?

By incorporating a gratitude journal into your daily routine, you can shift your focus towards positivity, increase your vibrational frequency, and attract more blessings into your life. Give it a try and see how it can transform your mindset and outlook on life.

Practice Mindfulness

Like keeping a gratitude journal, Meditation is a quick and effective way to increase your energy and raise your vibration.

Meditating after journaling about your blessings, aspirations, or powerful affirmations, in particular, can significantly impact your energy and mood, especially if you do so immediately afterward.

Accept Your Past And Yourself

Accepting your past and yourself is a fundamental step toward personal growth and emotional well-being. This journey involves recognizing and embracing your history, experiences, and the person you are today, which can lead to greater self-compassion and resilience.

The process of acceptance begins with acknowledging your past, including both the positive experiences and the challenges you may have faced. Every individual carries a unique story shaped by their upbringing, relationships, and life events. Rather than dwelling on regrets or mistakes, it's essential to understand that these experiences contribute to your growth and the person you have become. Embracing your past allows you to learn from it, fostering a sense of wisdom and strength that can guide you moving forward.

Self-acceptance is equally vital. Many people struggle with self-criticism, often comparing themselves unfavorably to others or striving for an unattainable ideal. To cultivate self-acceptance, it is crucial to treat yourself with kindness and compassion, recognizing that everyone has flaws and imperfections. Engaging in positive self-talk and reframing negative thoughts can help shift your mindset toward one that values authenticity and embraces your uniqueness.

Additionally, meditation and mindfulness practices can support the journey of acceptance. These techniques encourage you to remain present, observing your thoughts and emotions without judgment. By practicing mindfulness, you can develop a deeper understanding of yourself and create a safe space to process past experiences.

Accepting your past and yourself does not mean resigning to it; rather, it's about acknowledging your reality, learning from it, and using it as a foundation for future growth. By letting go of self-doubt and embracing who you are, you empower yourself to live authentically and fully engage in life's opportunities. Ultimately, acceptance leads to greater inner peace, stronger relationships, and a more fulfilling life.

"Acknowledge and accept"

Great manifestors are self-aware and even in love with their own abilities. They acknowledge and accept all of their mistakes and failures, continuing to move forward despite setbacks. Acceptance is the act of acknowledging and embracing reality as it is, without attempting to change or resist it. It involves letting go of the need to control outcomes and accepting things for what they are. Acceptance is an important part of personal growth and self-improvement, as it allows us to move past negative emotions and experiences and to focus on what we can control.

Loving yourself means treating yourself with kindness, compassion, and respect. It means accepting yourself for who you are, including your strengths and weaknesses, flaws and imperfections. Loving yourself involves practicing self-care, setting healthy boundaries, and taking responsibility for your own well-being.

Here are some ways you can practice acceptance and self-love:

1. Embrace your imperfections: Accept that you are not perfect, and that's okay. Everyone has flaws and weaknesses, and that's what makes us human. Embrace your imperfections and focus on your strengths.
2. Let go of control: Accept that there are some things you cannot control. Learn to let go of the need to control outcomes, and instead focus on what you can control, such as your thoughts and actions.
3. Practice self-compassion: Treat yourself with the same kindness and compassion you would offer to a friend. Acknowledge your own pain and struggles, and be gentle with yourself as you navigate difficult emotions and experiences.
4. Set healthy boundaries: Take care of yourself by setting healthy boundaries with others. This means learning to say "no" when you need to, and prioritizing your own well-being.
5. Practice self-care: Take care of yourself physically,

emotionally, and mentally. This might involve engaging in activities that bring you joy, getting enough sleep and exercise, and seeking support from others when you need it.

6. Celebrate your successes: Take time to acknowledge and celebrate your successes, no matter how small they may seem. Celebrating your successes can help boost your confidence and self-esteem.

Overall, acceptance and self-love are important aspects of personal growth and well-being. By practicing acceptance and self-love, you can learn to embrace who you are, live authentically, and cultivate greater happiness and fulfillment in your life.

Your ability to love yourself is the most powerful manifestation signal you can send out to the universe. While self-love is a process that may take some time, you can begin taking steps toward it right away.

Practicing self-care and engaging in activities that make you feel good does not have to be difficult or time-consuming to be effective. Even the smallest habits can lead to greater self-love and self-confidence, as well as an increase in your vibration. And the more love you have for yourself, the more love you will attract to yourself.

Follow Up On Small Goals And Prove Yourself

Manifesting something significant isn't any more difficult than manifesting a cup of coffee, for example. However, most people fail at manifesting because they attempt to attract things as large as a house or a large, unexpected payment without fully believing that they are capable of achieving their goals.

When you begin to doubt the law of attraction and the manifestation process, you are effectively putting it out of commission.

You cannot deceive the universe; it always delivers what you believe and feels. You cannot fool the universe. When you have a nagging doubt that something will work, you put measures to ensure that it will not.

To overcome these fears, beginning with small manifestations and demonstrating to yourself that it actually works is necessary before beginning to manifest large-scale changes.

Take An Inspired Action

Once you clearly understand what you want to attract, the next step is to take determined action. The universe will not work against you but rather with you.

The law of attraction can assist you in achieving your goals more quickly and easily. Still, you must first put in the necessary effort. Obviously, sitting on the couch all day eating ice cream while hoping for a healthy, lean body is not going to work, no matter how much you believe in it.

Using Law Of Attraction For Specific Goal

Low And Relationships

The first step in using the law of attraction to attract more love into your life is to become aware of any ways in which you might be subconsciously resisting it.

To give an example, according to Kaiser, "if the universe keeps sending you unavailable people, this could indicate that something within you is still unavailable."

Once you have identified this stumbling block, you can begin removing these internal barriers and developing a more open approach to interpersonal relationships. Consider who you truly are and what you want, and then trust that the universe will provide you with the partner you require, not necessarily the one you want or expect to receive.

Objectives In Professional Life

When using the law of attraction in your professional life, it's critical to be very specific about what you want to achieve.

Write down your professional aspirations in concrete terms, such as "I want to work with like-minded people who support my ideas" or "I earn X amount of money in X city." And, of course, action is critical in this situation. Consider the following question: "What would the 'promoted me do?" If you want that promotion, ask yourself: "What would the promoted-me do?"

For Your Finances

Financial anxieties are real and understandable. It takes a lot of unlearning to develop a positive relationship between financial abundance and abundance.

When it comes to money, it's especially easy to fall into a mindset of scarcity. As an alternative, make every effort to concentrate on what you already have rather than on what you lack. This is accomplished through the use of a mantra such as

"Abundance flows through me so I can happily give."

In all of these areas, it's best to start small and concentrate on bringing about small, manageable changes first. More practice will make you more effective at manifesting. Eventually, you'll be able to tackle more significant and life-altering changes.

Chapter 3: How The Law Of Attraction Can Improve Your Life

Since the book "The Secret" in 2006, psychologists, New Age thinkers, and religious leaders have been discussing the Law Of Attraction. However, it has only recently gained popularity again.

The law of attraction is as simple: we attract whatever we think about, whether good or bad.

Oprah is a supporter of the law. She devoted an episode of her show to discuss how it has the potential to change people's lives. Whether or not you believe in the power of the universe, there is scientific evidence that the effects of positive thinking can be seen in everyday life.

I've highlighted the most compelling aspects of the law of attraction for your consideration.

Positive Thoughts Can Attract Positive Experiences

Experiences

The idea that positive thoughts can attract positive experiences stems from the belief that our mindset and emotions significantly influence our reality. This concept, often linked to the "law of attraction," suggests that what we focus on grows. By maintaining a positive outlook, we create an environment that fosters happiness, success, and personal growth.

When we think positively, we approach life with optimism, resilience, and an open mind. These traits enable us to identify opportunities and navigate challenges with confidence. For instance, a person who believes in their ability to succeed is more likely to take proactive steps toward their goals, ultimately increasing their chances of achieving them.

Furthermore, positivity is contagious. When we exude optimism, we attract supportive, like-minded individuals who amplify our sense of well-being. This network of encouragement creates a cycle of positivity, where good energy flows in both directions.

On a deeper level, positive thoughts also influence our emotional and physical health. Optimistic individuals often experience lower stress levels, stronger immune systems, and greater life satisfaction. These benefits enhance our capacity to seize joyful experiences and embrace life's possibilities.

In essence, maintaining positive thoughts is a powerful tool for creating a fulfilling life. By focusing on gratitude, hope, and self-belief, we align ourselves with positive energy, inviting enriching experiences into our journey.

The person who speaks the most about illness is the one who is ill. The one who speaks of prosperity is the one who possesses prosperity. You are a magnet for everything. By concentrating on something, you can bring it about. positive thoughts attract positive experiences by creating a vibrational frequency that interacts with the energy of the universe. By focusing on positive thoughts, practicing gratitude, and visualizing our desired outcome, we can attract positive experiences, opportunities, and people into our lives. Remember, the power of positivity lies within us, and by harnessing it, we can create a happier and more fulfilling life.

When You Think Of Something Positive,

You Invite It To Your Life

When you think a small thought about something you want, the Law of Attraction causes that thought to grow larger and larger, as well as more and more powerful as time passes. In other words, keep your thoughts positive.

Concentration Makes Everything Powerful

Using this technique, you can create your own reality by "attracting" the experiences that you want to have in your life. According to the laws described in the book, you are most likely responsible for your own misfortune by being concerned about it too much.

Trust Your Emotions Rather Than Overthinking

Trusting your emotions can be a powerful tool for making decisions and navigating life, especially when overthinking leads to confusion or hesitation. Emotions are often instinctive, arising from deep-seated values and experiences, while overthinking involves a barrage of analysis that can cloud judgment and breed anxiety.

Emotions are the mind's natural way of signaling what feels right or wrong. They often stem from our subconscious, which processes information faster than conscious thought. For example, a sense of unease in a situation might indicate that something is not aligned with your values or safety. By trusting your emotional responses, you can tap into this intuitive wisdom.

Overthinking, on the other hand, tends to overcomplicate situations. While logical reasoning is important, excessive analysis can lead to paralysis by analysis, where you are stuck evaluating every possible outcome without making a decision. This can prevent progress and even increase stress.

Trusting your emotions also fosters authenticity. When you honor how you feel, you stay true to yourself and your needs, rather than overanalyzing to fit external expectations. This self-awareness can improve relationships, as it helps you communicate your feelings honestly and set healthy boundaries.

Of course, it's important to balance emotions with rational thought. However, learning to listen to your inner voice and trust your instincts can often provide clarity and direction where overthinking fails. By embracing your emotions, you empower yourself to act confidently and live more authentically.

In other words, pay attention to your gut feeling. Instead of overthinking your decisions, allow your emotions to guide you toward what is right and wrong for you. As a result, you will have a more fulfilling life.

Accelerate The Power Of Manifestation

Through Concentration

It is possible to have a desire and/or a need for something when you are experiencing positive emotion and want to focus your attention or give thought to that something. When you devote your full attention to a subject and feel only positive emotions toward it while doing so, the subject will enter your experience very quickly. Manifesting through concentration is a powerful technique that involves focusing your thoughts and energy on a specific goal or desire. This technique is based on the law of attraction, which states that we can attract what we focus on into our lives. By concentrating our thoughts and energy on a desired outcome, we can manifest it into reality.

To begin manifesting through concentration, it is important to first identify your desired outcome. This can be anything from a new job or relationship to improved health or financial abundance. Once you have identified your desired outcome, focus your thoughts and energy on it, visualizing yourself already having achieved it.

To enhance your concentration, it can be helpful to practice meditation or deep breathing exercises. These techniques can help calm your mind and allow you to focus more deeply on your desired outcome.

It is also important to maintain a positive mindset and believe that your desired outcome is possible. Negative thoughts and self-doubt can create resistance and interfere with the process of manifestation. Instead, focus on the positive aspects of your desired outcome and trust that the universe will bring it to you in the best possible way.

Finally, take inspired action towards your desired outcome. This can involve setting specific goals, taking steps towards achieving them, and remaining open to opportunities that come your way. By taking action towards your goal, you show the universe that you are ready to receive your desired outcome.

In conclusion, manifesting through concentration involves focusing your thoughts and energy on a specific goal or desire, visualizing yourself already having achieved it, and taking inspired action towards your goal. By using this technique, you can manifest your desires into reality and create the life you truly want. Remember to maintain a positive mindset, take action towards your goals, and trust in the process of manifestation.

Imagine Things The Way You Want Them

To Be To See The Changes

This is something that successful people are aware of. It is also referred to as visualization. Michael Phelps stated that he visualizes himself winning every night before going to bed.

For true positive change to occur in your life, you must first disregard the way things are and the way other people see and perceive you — and devote more of your time and attention to the way you would prefer things to be.

Powerful Positive Thinking Can Attract

More Positive Things

Spend 15 minutes every day reflecting on your life goals, dreams, and what you want to achieve in your endeavors. This improves your chances of being successful.

Keep In Mind That You Can Be Successful

The fact that others are successful does not preclude your own success. According to the book, by attracting abundance to yourself, you are not limiting the opportunities of others.

Don't Be Depressed Because Of Your Failure

Being disappointed only serves to attract more things to be disappointed about. It is a clear indication that you are not getting what you want in life. So instead of focusing on what you don't have, consider how you can obtain what you desire.

Stay Away From Shows That Encourage

Negative Thoughts

Allowing this to enter your system makes you think about it more. It increases the likelihood that it will happen to you. Anything that attracts your attention is being drawn closer to you. Watching negative movies and being around negative people can definitely have an impact on our thoughts, emotions, and overall energy. Negativity can create a sense of heaviness and drain our energy, making it difficult to focus on positive thoughts and manifest the things we desire.

Negative movies and media can plant negative thoughts and images in our minds, which can impact our subconscious and ultimately affect our beliefs and actions. It is important to be aware of the content we consume and how it affects us. If a certain movie or media is leaving you feeling drained, anxious or stressed, it may be best to avoid it.

Similarly, being around negative people can also impact our energy and well-being. Negative people tend to complain, criticize, and focus on the negative aspects of situations. This can create a sense of negativity in the environment, which can affect the people around them. It is important to surround ourselves with positive and supportive people who uplift us and inspire us to be our best selves.

In contrast, being around positive people and watching uplifting movies can have a positive impact on our energy and mindset. Positive people tend to inspire, encourage, and focus on the positive aspects of situations. This can create a sense of positivity and upliftment, which can help us stay focused on our goals and manifest the things we desire.

In summary, it is important to be aware of the content we consume and the people we surround ourselves with. Negative movies and media can impact our thoughts and beliefs, while negative people can drain our energy and affect our mindset. It is important to focus on positivity, surround ourselves with positive people, and consume uplifting content that supports our goals and desires.

Understand That You Are The Architect Of Your Life And Relationships

Personal relationships can be ruined if you spend all of your time thinking about the negative. This way of thinking can assist us in escaping from toxic relationships with family members or a spouse. Nothing can enter your experience unless you are attracted to it on a personal level, to begin with.

Use Your Dreams As A Guide

Even though dreams can provide some insight into one's personality, you are not in the process of "creating" while you are sleeping.

Chapter 4: The Science Behind The

Law Of Attraction

My graduation day, which took place on April 25th, is one of my fondest memories. The student who had won the award for the best all-rounder for the postgraduate class of 2010 was to be announced by the master of ceremonies during the ceremony. A cash prize of $1,500 was also awarded as part of the award.

I was optimistic about winning the championship because I had worked extremely hard and had visualized the entire scenario numerous times. The practice of "mental rehearsal," as scientists refer to it, is something that performers engage in quite frequently before a show. I had no intention of performing anything here. Still, I had every intention of creating an event that I had imagined in my mind before arriving.

My irrational thought came to fruition, to my surprise. As I walked up to the stage to accept the award, I found myself reliving each and every moment that I had previously imagined in my imagination. This experience left a lasting impression on my consciousness, and tracing its origins has become a lifelong quest.

Dr. Joseph Murphy's book The Power of Your Subconscious Mind was the first book that introduced me to the concept of manifesting your desires. For a complete novice like myself, the notion that our subconscious mind can manifest whatever we imagine was a revolutionary concept. I experienced a complete shift in my thinking after reading The Secret by Rhonda Bryne, learning about the deep ancient wisdom and amazing experience of pranic healing, and learning about the work of visionaries

31

such as Dr. Bruce Lipton, Joe Dispenza, and Paramahansa Yogananda. I found fulfillment in assisting individuals and organizations in implementing this simple yet powerful concept.

At its core, the concept of the Law of Attraction is an ancient concept that has been incorporated into universal laws. It asserts that we are the architects of our own lives. We, as a collective consciousness, can influence and create the events of our life. Many of us have already had the experience of seeing something that we had imagined come to life. Almost every major religion, in some form or another, speaks about this concept.

The theory of quantum mechanics provides a plausible explanation for the feasibility of this law. The Nobel Prize-winning physicist Max Planck, who was one of the founding fathers of quantum physics, once said, "As a man who has devoted his entire life to the most objective science known to man, the study of matter, I can tell you as a result of my atom-related research that there is no such thing as matter! Nothing exists without the existence of a force, which is responsible for causing the vibration of the atom's particles and holding this atom's most minute solar system together... We must consider the possibility of the existence of a conscious and intelligent Mind as the source of this force. This Mind is the structural framework of all matter."

A person or entity with an infinite and intelligent mind is what our forefathers referred to as "infinite consciousness." Because we are considered to be part of infinite and powerful consciousness, it is believed that we can influence matter and bring our desires to fruition. This revelation is supported by several research studies conducted on prayer, which has proven an extremely effective tool for manifestation. According to one study, women who had been prayed for had a pregnancy rate nearly twice as high as that of women who had not received prayer. In another study, which involved 22 bush babies, it was discovered that the animals who were prayed for had a greater improvement in wound size compared to the animals who were not prayed for.

René Peoc'h, a French researcher, conducted another study that yielded some interesting findings. A self-propelled robot was used during the experiment, which normally wandered around a room aimlessly and randomly. When a cage containing live chicks was introduced, they took to the robot as if it were their mother. The robot began to spend more time in the area closer to the chicks as a result. Peoc'h concluded that the chicks' desire to remain close to the robot (whom they perceived to be their mother) manifested itself in a dramatic change in the robot's movements.

Let's take a look at some simple ways to put this powerful concept into practice to see positive changes in our lives.

- Establish a clear picture of your desired outcome. This step is analogous to the foundation of a building: nothing can stand on its own without it. You must be crystal clear about the outcome you seek and the intention behind achieving that outcome. There should be no hazy notions about it floating around in your head. Your desired outcome must be represented by an image in your mind.

• Put yourself in a state of gratitude. The goal of "GIGS," as I like to refer to it, is to harness the power of gratitude. Gratitude can increase one's energy. It puts

us in a powerful manifestation state, which is extremely beneficial. The key is to cultivate gratitude for people, events, and things for which you are truly grateful. Every day, set aside 10 minutes to write about your experiences.

• Create a mental picture of what you want. Begin visualizing the outcome as soon as you have a clear intention and feel grateful for the process. The steps should be carried out seamlessly. The visualization should be so realistic that you feel like you are actually experiencing the event in the present moment. You should be able to feel the emotional and mental intensity of its occurrence. In the same way that you can recall a frightening thought and feel the fear, you can also recall a beautiful experience and feel good.

• Recognize your defeat and accept your fate. You have no choice but to submit, come hell or high water. You must relinquish control of the outcome to higher intelligence. This will assist you in detaching. As a result, you won't have to deal with any anxiety or doubt during the process. Faith is capable of moving mountains.

• These are four simple steps that anyone can follow to manifest anything in their lives. Practice them regularly until you have mastered them, just like any other skill.

According to Einstein, "The power of imagination cannot be overstated. It serves as a preview of the attractions that will be available later in life." It's time to get creative. Albert Einstein's quote about the power of imagination highlights the importance of using our imagination to manifest our desires and create the life we want. Imagination is a powerful tool that allows us to visualize and create a mental picture of the things we want in our lives.

When we imagine something, we create a mental image that can be a preview of the attractions that will be presented to us in the future. This mental image can help us prepare for or anticipate what's coming next, and it can also allow us to explore different scenarios and possibilities in our minds.

When we imagine something, our brain creates neural patterns that are similar to those that occur when we actually experience the thing we're imagining. This is why imagining something can feel so real and vivid, even though it's not actually happening in the moment.

Imagination can also be a powerful tool for problem-solving, creativity, and innovation. By imagining new possibilities and ways of doing things, we can come up with novel solutions to challenges and innovate in different areas of our lives.

Overall, imagination is a vital cognitive ability that allows us to simulate experiences in our minds, explore new ideas and possibilities, and prepare for future events.

Chapter 5: How The Power Of

Visualization Can Help Achieve Your Goals

Isn't it interesting to consider what Olympic athletes are thinking about just before they compete? Consider the following scenario: they're speaking in front of thousands, perhaps even millions, of people. While they're watching their competition and thinking about all the things that could go wrong and how to avoid them, they're also feeling nervous.

This sounds reasonable, doesn't it? After all, that's most likely what we would do if we were in their shoes. Though it is important to visualize mistakes, well-trained athletes understand that they should never do so, especially right before a competition. Why? This is because visualizing mistakes or poor performance before an event increases the likelihood that athletes will actually do those things during the event, even if they don't intend to.

As a result, most top athletes are taught to visualize their desired outcomes just before competition begins. They imagine themselves as the winner of the game, the person who runs the fastest race, or the person who scores the winning point. Rather than visualizing what they do not want to happen, they are taught to "imagine" what they do want to happen. As a result of doing so, their chances of success skyrocket dramatically.

This is the power of visualization – and you, too, can employ this technique daily to assist you in achieving your objectives and fulfilling your dreams. This article will discuss what visualization

36

is and how you can begin incorporating it into your daily routine.

What Is The Power Of Visualization?

Visualization is a simple technique that you can use to create a strong mental image of a future event. It can be used to create a strong mental image of a future event. You can practice for the event in advance if you make good use of visualization techniques, which will allow you to prepare properly for it. Furthermore, by visualizing success, you can develop the self-confidence necessary to perform at your best.

Consider the following scenario: you have a major job interview scheduled for next week. You're already feeling nervous, and it's easy to be concerned about giving poor answers to the interviewer's questions, speaking awkwardly about your previous accomplishments, or forgetting to bring your letters of recommendation with you to the interview.

Is this something you've heard before? This type of negative thinking is probably something we've all experienced.

In this case, instead of thinking negatively, you could use visualization to imagine that the interview went smoothly. You could imagine yourself speaking confidently, effortlessly describing all of your previous accomplishments, and providing letters of recommendation to the interviewer as part of your preparation. Isn't it true that your vision is much clearer now?

The Advantages Of Visulization

Visualizing the outcomes that you desire can help you feel more confident. "Seeing" yourself succeed encourages you to believe that it is possible – and will occur.

When you visualize success, you can "practice" success. When you visualize every step of an event or activity going smoothly, you prepare your mind and body for the actual steps to be taken in that event or activity.

Visualization can be beneficial to anyone at any time. A life coach or personal development expert is not required to use visualization techniques to achieve personal development goals. Visualization, or the process of creating mental images, can have many advantages. Here are some of them:

1. Improved performance: Visualization has been shown to improve performance in a variety of activities, from sports to public speaking. By visualizing yourself succeeding at a task, you can increase your confidence and motivation, and improve your ability to execute the task successfully.

2. Reduced anxiety and stress: Visualization can be a helpful tool for reducing anxiety and stress. By visualizing calming scenes or positive outcomes, you can train your mind to focus on positive thoughts and reduce negative feelings.

3. Increased creativity: Visualization can help stimulate creativity by allowing you to explore new possibilities and ideas. By visualizing different scenarios or outcomes, you can generate new ideas and find innovative solutions to problems.

4. Better decision-making: Visualization can help you

make better decisions by allowing you to simulate different scenarios and outcomes in your mind. By visualizing the potential consequences of different choices, you can make more informed decisions.

5. Improved memory: Visualization can help improve memory by creating stronger neural connections in the brain. By visualizing information you want to remember, you can help your brain encode and retain that information more effectively.

Overall, visualization can be a powerful tool for personal growth, problem-solving, and performance improvement in a variety of areas.

Steps To Practicing Visualization

Decide What You Want To Do

What do you want to put your attention on? Choose one dream or goal to focus on and begin visualizing it. Consider, for example, visualizing a successful outcome of the presentation you'll be giving the following week.

Visualize The Situation In Your Head

Start picturing the exact scene in your mind. Don't be vague or unclear – the more specific you are, and the more specific the details you imagine, the more effective the visualization will be in helping you.

Imagine yourself in the situation as if you were there. What color are the walls, by the way? What kind of clothes are you wearing? Who else is present in the room with you?

Keep in mind that you should engage all of your senses during the visualization exercise. Include all of your senses – sight, sound, taste, smell, and touch – so that you can truly bring your vision to life.

Consider the following scenario: you are standing in front of a group of people. Imagine the expressions on the faces of each team member, as well as what each person is wearing. Hear the sound of papers being moved around, smell the aroma of freshly brewed coffee, and take in the sight of the sun streaming through the windows of the office.

Also, imagine how you're feeling and what you're going through. You're excited and confident about the presentation you're about to give, and you're ready to go. Knowing that your team members will enjoy hearing what you have to say and benefit from the information you share with them gives you great confidence. You're looking forward to getting started with your project.

Take Small Steps Towards A Successful

Conclusion

What actions will you need to take to ensure that your presentation is a success?

Determine each step that must be completed for you to achieve your goal. And as part of your visualization exercise, begin picturing each step in detail.

For example, the introduction to your presentation will be the first part of the presentation. As a result, visualize yourself explaining to the group why you're giving the presentation and what they can expect to gain from it.

Consider the talking points you'll use and what you'll say for each slide as you prepare your presentation. Visualize your hand motions, and imagine looking directly at everyone as you speak to help you remember your points.

Consider going over the entire presentation in your head, paying attention to each step and how you'll feel. Always remember to concentrate on what you want rather than on what you don't want. When you're taking a test, you want to be relaxed and confident, not nervous or forgetful. As a result, concentrate on the positive emotions and avoid the negative ones.

Practice Visualization Daily

If your presentation is two weeks away, make a point of doing a complete visualization at least once a day until the big day.

It is critical to be consistent with your visualization because regular visualization can train your brain to believe that what you imagine is actually the truth. It's true that the more you visualize something, the stronger that vision becomes – and the greater the likelihood that you'll receive what you desire. Why? Because you've already completed the task.

Visualizing daily is similar to training for a marathon or improving one's golf swing. You will become more familiar with those specific "motions" the more you practice, and your body (or your mind) will become more familiar with them. You're literally putting in the work to prepare your mind for a positive outcome.

The beauty of visualization is that it can be done anywhere at any time: on the train to and from work, before going to bed at night, or while drinking your morning cup of coffee.

Why Visualization Is Effective

According to research conducted with brain imagery, visualization works because neurons in our brains, those electrically excitable cells that transmit information, interpret imagery as being equivalent to a real-life action. When we visualize a movement, the brain generates an impulse that instructs our neurons to "perform" the movement in our bodies.

In turn, this establishes a new neural pathway — a network of cells in our brain that collaborate to form memories or learn new behaviors — that prepares our body to behave in a manner consistent with our imagination. This occurs without the need to engage in any physical activity. Still, the result is the same as if the activity were performed.

Visualization Exercise To Practice

• Select a location with plenty of peace and quiet. Prepare for your visualization exercises in a quiet environment. The ability to concentrate on the experience and reap the maximum benefit from it is enhanced in this way. The amount of time it takes to get back into the full visualization increases with each interruption you experience.

• Make a single sentence that describes the outcome you want to achieve. Make a note of this statement and place it somewhere visible, such as on or near your desk. This keeps the positive outcome in front of you, where you'll be reminded of it regularly, which is beneficial. If possible, repeat the sentence aloud several times throughout the day.

• Figure out what kind of image you want to represent your visualization. Our presentation example could be a picture of someone who is confidently speaking in front of a group of people. Place this image somewhere that will be easily visible to you – on your desk, as your computer's wallpaper, or somewhere else. This is yet another tool that can assist you in visualizing your desired outcome while you're at your desk.

Chapter 6: The Mindset Of A

Successful Person

What is a Successful Mindset? Your first step to developing a successful mindset is to know what one is. When you define a mindset for success, it seems simpler than it actually is. For example, the definition of a successful mindset is someone who is willing to accept success and take advantage of opportunities. Many of you might be thinking, "Well, that's me! I'm willing to accept success. I'll take advantage of an opportunity if it comes along." But don't let the simplicity of the definition fool you because there is much more to it than the literality behind these words. For example, you might think that you are willing to accept success, but most people aren't. Some people want success, but they don't think that they deserve it, they don't think they are smart enough to achieve it, and they lack confidence in themselves as a successful person. In addition, those same people who think that they would take advantage of an opportunity if it came along have already passed by dozens of opportunities that might have resulted in their success if they were willing to put in the work. What they really meant was – I'll take advantage of an opportunity if I don't have to do a lot of work. The Successful Mindset Difference The difference between a successful mindset and one that just wants success is how much work they are willing to put into the effort to get success. It all comes down to how much you believe in what you are doing and how passionate you are about it. For example, someone who is passionate about their business and believes that they will be able to be successful at it may spend hours working

44

on it that other people might spend watching television, going out on the town or hanging with their friends. Some successful people have been able to make their bones while still working a full-time job to support their family. This means that they had to work on their business or income streams while everyone else was enjoying leisure time. This is very common in the case of a novelist who suddenly makes it big. Odds are, they were slaving away at the computer for years while so-called aspiring writers were watching The Bachelor. How to Develop a Successful Mindset So, how do you actually develop this successful mindset? Well, it involves a process with many steps and if you are like most people, you are going to have to start at the bottom. You'll start with step one and when you have mastered it, you'll move onto the next step. However, keep in mind that it takes time to completely change your mindset. You have had the same basic mindset for success for many years and it can be difficult to change at first. That's why using daily habits to change your mindset is the number one strategy used by the business world. Here are the steps for creating a mindset for success: 1. Give yourself permission to succeed: Many people just don't believe that they should have the success that they desire, so their own mind actually keeps them from getting there. Maybe they feel guilty because of past mistakes, or do not think that their religious or moral beliefs will permit them to have a great deal of money. Whatever the reason, you first need to give yourself permission to succeed or else you won't even be able to start the journey. 2. Believe in your ability to succeed: Just as important as giving yourself permission to succeed is the belief that you have what it takes to be successful. Everyone has something that they are good at, and some of the people you would never think could have made a success of themselves because of physical health, mental illness, financial difficulties, lack of education or other circumstances, have become some of the most well-known success stories of our time. 3. Take care of Yourself: Research conducted into the personal habits of some of the richest and most powerful people in the world who have achieved success on their own show certain trends that are far too common to be coincidence. Successful people take better care of themselves than the average person does. They sleep better at night, with most getting between 6 and 10 hours, they exercise regularly and stay in shape, and they eat health most of the time. 4. Set Goals for Yourself: So, you want to be successful. How are you going to achieve it? Setting goals and creating a plan for success is often what separates the average person from the very successful one. The average person might know that they want to be successful, but they have no plan to get there. Just as ineffective as having no goals at all is something that many people do - setting goals that have no clear path to achievement. For example, one of these goals might be: I want to be rich in 10 years. 5. Keep Track of Your Progress: You should also be tracking your progress every day or week to determine how you are coming with your plans for success. Even if you aren't doing as well as you should be, you still want to write down what you have achieved. There are a couple of reasons for this: first of all, you will be able to look back and see how much success you have achieved and be motivated to continue reaching for your goals. Second, you can easily see where you need to make adjustments in your plan when you have tracked it over a period of time. 6. Concentrate on the Things That Matter: If you want to be successful then you don't want to waste your time on things that aren't going to give you success or are not working out the way you had intended. Successful people know when to fold their hand and leave the table to try a different game and you should avoid continuing futile efforts when you are fairly certain that you aren't going to reap any benefits from them. Of course, that doesn't mean to jump ship at the first sign of trouble, but it does mean being aware when you have reached the point when you just need to move on. 7. Be all you can be: If you aren't going to give 100% of your effort to the task of being successful then one of two things are going to happen: one, you aren't going to achieve the level of success that you want at all, or two, you are going to take a lot longer getting there than you should have. If you are going to write a book, start a business or work in the ever growing internet marketing industry, make sure that you are giving it your best effort and don't hold back. 8. Be Flexible: One thing that you will learn as you start the journey towards success is that things are almost never going to go according to plan. If you create a set-in-stone goal and milestone list and then try to achieve them, you are always going to fail unless you are able to be flexible. Anything might happen that could derail your efforts and you need to be able to roll with the punches and continue the journey even when your original plan didn't work out. For example, suppose that you planned to train for a marathon this summer, but ended up breaking your leg. You need to change your plan and figure out some other way that you can work towards your success, and then come back to the marathon training at a later date when you are healed up. 9. Develop Daily Habits That Stick: When you want to be successful, you need to understand up front that it is a long journey. Everyone proceeds at a different pace, but the number one thing that you can do to speed things up is to develop habits for success and make them stick. Habits like getting up early, getting enough sleep, putting all of your efforts into your work, saving money and learning as much as you can will help you shape your future and make your success come much quicker. 10. Don't Remove Bad Habits, Replace Them: If you have bad habits that you are trying to get rid of, keep in mind that you will have a much better chance of doing that if you replace them with good habits instead. For example, if you are trying to change a bad habit of eating fast food for lunch on a daily basis, you will have much better results if you try to make eating healthy a daily habit rather than attempting to get rid of eating unhealthy. Other Ways to Develop a Successful Mindset If you want to develop the kind of mindset that you need for financial success or any other type of success that you are trying to create in your life, then you should start by learning as much as you can about certain aspects of psychological development that pertains to successful mindsets: namely, cultivating habits, setting goals, working with others and many other subjects. One of the things that you can do that will help you a great deal is to study what other successful people that you admire are doing, and how they were able to get to where they are today. Many successful people have biographies or autobiographies that will give you lots of good information as to how they were able to achieve their success and how you can model your own efforts after theirs. You also need to decide what is most important to you and have a clear picture of it in your mind. Success comes in many different forms. For example, some people seek after financial success while others want their work to be recognized and consumed by the masses. Whether you are starting the next dotcom revolution or you are writing the Great American Novel, you want to have your end goal first and foremost in your mind. A successful mindset is only the first step in achieving success. This is also something that you need to bear in mind. The hard work actually comes after you prepare yourself and set your goals ñ the part where you put forth the effort that will be required in order to achieve those goals. The most important thing to remember is that you need to believe in yourself and in your ability to be successful. There are people out there who have more education than you; people who have more money to invest into a business than you do and people who have plenty more free time than you do to work on their success. But that doesn't mean that you cannot have the things that you desire. Your specific circumstances have very little to do with how much success you will be able to achieve. Instead, how motivated you are and willing you are to put forth the effort will determine how far you get. Advantages like money and time can certainly be a big help, but the most important factor in determining if you will be successful if how bad you want it. Success is a game of the mind. If you don't believe me, just take a look around you.

There are many people out there who have extraordinary talent, passion, and mad skills. Still, they aren't crushing it in business or winning in life as a result. Do you know a talented web designer or coach who is struggling to make ends meet these days?

Perhaps you're friends with an incredibly successful and driven entrepreneur who is unable to make ends meet. You may be that talented but unpromising individual. Some of you may be thinking to yourself, "I know I have the abilities to succeed, but I have no idea how I'm going to pay the bills this month." When it comes to rising to the top, talent, skills, and passion are only a small part of the overall strategy. What about the rest? It all comes down to your frame of mind.

Here are four of the most powerful mindset characteristics that successful people have in common. Take a look at them. Then make the most of the ones you have while working on the ones you don't.

Make Sure To Always Take The First Step

And "Start" Your Tasks

You have everything you need to achieve your objectives. You're motivated, and you're ready to go. You're not bothered by the effort required to get there. Quite the contrary, you're looking forward to it.

As a result, when new and exciting projects and collaborations come across your desk, you say yes to them all. You believe that being successful is defined by having a slew of incredible projects running simultaneously. I'm sorry to be the one to break it to you, but that isn't correct.

Truly successful people are meticulous in their selection of the projects on which they will collaborate. Their primary focus is on seeing things through to completion and completing what they begin. It doesn't matter how good the project is or how brilliant the idea is; if you don't finish what you start, you won't see any results or make any significant strides forward in your life or business.

Keep in mind that going all out for one or two excellent projects is preferable to going half-hearted on a hundred excellent projects. Always.

Always Strive For Continuous Improvement

Dr. Carol S. Dweck, a Stanford University psychologist and author of "Mindset: Changing the Way You Think to Fulfill Your Potential," explains that successful people have a growth mindset.

A growth mindset is characterized by the belief that achieving success results from making continuous, consistent progress. To achieve success, you must first understand that it is an ongoing process rather than an endpoint in itself. This implies that you are always willing to learn and improve to achieve your objectives.

Successful people have a growth mindset, and they are content to keep trying until they achieve their objectives. Their willingness to experiment with various strategies and techniques stems from their conviction that doing so will eventually get them where they want to go... And they're absolutely correct.

Develop Confidence In Your Own Skills

This one is all about putting your negative beliefs on the shelf and walking away. Before you can succeed, you must first believe that you can. This is because your beliefs have an impact on your outer behaviors and actions.

When you have a strong belief in your ability to succeed, it is natural for you to direct your attention away from problems and toward solutions instead. Suppose you have negative beliefs about yourself and your ability to achieve your goals. In that case, it will be nearly impossible for you to accomplish what you set out to do.

Whatever path you take to reach your destination, you will face a steep uphill climb throughout the entire process. Every victory will be felt as if it were a hard-fought victory in a war. Every obstacle will seem insurmountable then. The majority of people give up long before they reach the summit.

Those who are successful avoid falling into this trap because they can take actions consistent with their positive internal beliefs. They can get up off the couch and take the appropriate actions that will help them become super achievers in their fields. Those who do not believe they are capable of overcoming obstacles will not even attempt it. They are already out of the game before it has even begun.

Accept Who You Are

Successful people are aware of their own identities. They are completely aware of their objectives and aspirations. They are aware of their own personal values, as well as their own skills and abilities. They are also extremely candid about their flaws, which is refreshing. They don't try to be amazing at everything, and they don't pretend to be someone they aren't to appear successful.

If you despise parties and networking events, perhaps staying at home and participating in online events would be the best option for you. For those who are certain they will not be able to navigate the uncertainty of entrepreneurship, it may be best to work for someone they admire and trust that this is the path that will bring them the most joy and fulfillment.

When it comes to achieving long-term success, high achievers never lose sight that they must first master their own mindset.

All of your other incredible personality traits and skills will come together to propel you to your destination if you make a concerted effort to improve your mindset.

Chapter 7: Daily Lifestyle Habits Of

A Successful Person

We can all recognize a successful person when we see one, but what happens behind the scenes is often overlooked. Every one of the savvy investors, successful businessmen, and A-list celebrities we've come to admire has its own personal routines and systems, some of which are more bizarre than others in their personal lives. While authors Leo Tolstoy and Ludwig van Beethoven chose to forego money to make their own shoes, composer Ludwig van Beethoven began each day by hand-counting 60 coffee beans to make the perfect cup of coffee, this does not imply that it will work for you. The ability to balance routine and reward is unique to each individual, making it a difficult task to achieve.

Although the habits of successful people are a mixed bag, some consistent patterns can be observed across the board. From these, you can lay the groundwork for a happy and fulfilled life. You are what you repeatedly do. Suppose you change up your day-to-day to incorporate these success habits into your routine. In that case, you will see results in a very short period. Suppose you want to make a new activity a true part of your everyday life. In that case, it can take anywhere from 21 to 66 days of deliberate effort. Keep checking in, and we'll see you on the other side.

54

Try To Get Up In The Morning Without

An Alarm

There has never been a day that began with sleep. That is a proven fact. However, a significant number of days have been lost to sleep. If you can master your body clock and consistently hit those 6 a.m. wake-up calls, you'll be well on your way to crushing every day of your life. On the other hand, if you have developed the habit of snoozing your alarm, you may wake up feeling groggy and unmotivated in the morning.

Jeff Bezos, the CEO of Amazon and former world's richest man, is said to refuse to set the alarm each night to ensure that he gets at least eight hours of sleep, regardless of the time. In a similar vein, media mogul Arianna Huffington does not subscribe to the notion that an alarm clock is necessary. According to Huffington in an interview with CNBC, "just think about the definition of the word alarm," which is "a sudden fear or distressing suspense caused by an awareness of imminent danger."

Historically, rising early in the morning has been a favorite habit of successful individuals. Apparently, French composer Erik Satie arose at 7:18 a.m. on the dot, ate lunch at 12:11 p.m. on the dot, and ate dinner at 7:16 p.m. on the dot to ensure that his body clock was running at peak performance.

Even though this may seem absurd, there is some validity to the success habit. Starting the day without an alarm and establishing a routine allows you to ease into the day without being overwhelmed by the flood of stress hormones that you are accustomed to experiencing. Whatever method you use to get you out of bed in the morning, make sure you meet it halfway by going to bed at a reasonable hour. Maybe you shouldn't have that coffee at 4 p.m.

Make Sure To Read More

If you don't use your brain as a muscle, it will begin to deteriorate. While getting sucked into a good book is an excellent way to pass the time and has numerous benefits, self-help, non-fiction, and improvement books are where you'll really see the most significant improvements in your cognitive abilities.

During a recent interview with CNBC, investor Warren Buffett revealed that he begins every morning by reading the newspaper. He estimates that he spends at least 80 percent of his day doing so. "I read 500 pages a day like this, seven days a week. That is how knowledge functions. It accumulates in the same way that compound interest does. "I guarantee that not many of you will do it," he said, referring to the fact that everyone is capable of doing it.

Perhaps you should start making weekly visits to your local library a mandatory part of your schedule. Whatever method you find most effective for getting books to you, remember how hungry your brain is for more information; it literally wants to do nothing else but learn; therefore, allow it to play every now and then.

Make Sure To Workout And Exercise

Exercise is one of the most difficult parts of your day to avoid. Every casual gym-goer has thought to themselves, "I'll do it tomorrow." Still, if you don't set aside a specific time to work on your body, it will fail you one day. Successful people will carve out that time for themselves.

Take, for example, Bill Gates, the founder of Microsoft. In addition to watching DVDs during his morning treadmill workouts, the tech wizard and philanthropist is said to enjoy multitasking while working out.

Focus On Yourself For 15-20 Minutes Daily

Taking a brief break from the intense, over-sensory world we live in is a habit recommended by almost every success guide we reviewed. In a year, creating a calm space where you can engage in the kind of deep thought that is required to make a genuine change in your life will pay dividends tenfold in terms of personal growth.

LinkedIn CEO Jeff Weiner expresses his enthusiasm for meditation in his frequent tweets, claiming that the practice allows him to strategize and work more proactively. "Creating time to think, rather than constantly reacting, is a key component of time management," Weiner explained in an interview with The Wall Street Journal.

While putting this aside to make time for others may appear more 'productive' in the short term, it is a surefire way to burn out in the long term. When it comes to life, it's similar to how it is on airplanes: you must first take care of yourself before you can help anyone else.

Organize, Plan And Execute Everything

Strategically

Critical thinking is a man's best friend in the truest sense. Whatever you think of the thumb as a dividing line between beast and man, knowing where to put it has always been an important part of our evolution from ape-like creatures. Apply that same problem-solving ability to the issues you encounter daily. You will almost certainly achieve success.

When faced with a challenge, you wouldn't just charge headlong into it without thinking. Sit back and take the time to figure out the magnitude of the problem you're facing, as well as which foot you should use to jump off. The importance of planning cannot be overstated in the story of any success. Making it a habit is a huge step toward realizing your own success in the long run.

Surround Yourself People Who Inspire

You

We've probably all heard by now that our incomes are most likely the average of the incomes of our five closest friends. We naturally gravitate toward those with whom we have the most in common. Suppose you flip that notion on its head and begin surrounding yourself with mentors, idols, and inspirational figures. In that case, you will learn everything you need to know to succeed. For as long as you are providing something in return, it is a given that this will result in unexpected and unexpectedly beneficial improvements.

Seneca, the Roman philosopher, once said, "Luck is what happens when preparation and opportunity come together." Surrounding yourself with people who are full of inspiration can open the door to that opportunity.

Have personal Objectives And Pursue Them

The ability to turn dreams into reality is an absolute must-have in the skill set of anyone who wants to be successful. I have never experienced such joy as when I am taking a concept from its home, inside your head, and chipping away at every little bit of it until I have a tangible, existent object.

The establishment of specific personal objectives is critical in this process. Perhaps you require a notebook, a planner, or a whiteboard to complete your task. However, writing down your objectives in a visible location will serve as a reminder to you to continue working towards them, as well as a confirmation that the simple act of putting pen to paper has already begun the process of turning ideas into reality.

Have Different Sources Of Income

Never put all of your eggs in one basket at the same time. It's an oldie, but a goodie in my book. With the phrase, "gig-based economy" being uttered every third word on the news, diversifying your income has emerged as the hot new thing to be hailed as a golden step on the road to financial independence and financial security. Building your skills and then acting on your newly acquired and improved skill set are critical to success.

It's also never too late to start saving and investing. However, proceed with caution.

Be Frugal, Not Strict

When it comes to being frugal and stingy, there is a world of difference. Frugality is a learned behavior based on the principle of not spending money unnecessarily. Stinginess is a miserly attachment to money based solely on the hope of amassing a large enough collection of gold coins to take a bath in.

Frugal people are also successful. They are frugal with their money; they bargain, plan, and put money aside. To this end, creating and following a budget is an excellent first step toward achieving true financial independence. Beyond that, don't be afraid to spend money because it is an essential part of the world in which we live. Simply put, do not spend money that you do not have.

Always Share Your Work

Keep in mind that we're all in this together. Whatever your definition of success is, don't be embarrassed or afraid to share it with the rest of the world. You will inspire others through your work, and you will open the door to many opportunities for inspiration in return. Once you've demonstrated that you're committed to improving yourself, the offers to assist you will pour in. The following is how Chris Rock puts it more elegantly than we could:

"I'd always end up getting stuck on the side of the road." Nobody came to my aid when I was standing there trying to flag them down. While driving my own car, other drivers would get out and assist me in pushing the vehicle. If you want help, help yourself first – people appreciate it when they see it." There are many lifestyle habits that successful people practice on a daily basis. Here are some common ones:

1. Goal-setting: Successful people set clear and achievable goals for themselves, and work towards them every day.
2. Time-management: They manage their time effectively by prioritizing tasks, setting schedules and deadlines, and avoiding distractions.
3. Regular exercise: Successful people prioritize their physical health by exercising regularly, which helps them maintain their energy, focus, and overall wellbeing.
4. Continuous learning: They are always learning and seeking new knowledge and skills, whether through reading, attending seminars, or taking courses.
5. Positive mindset: Successful people maintain a positive mindset and focus on solutions, rather than dwelling on problems.
6. Networking: They build and maintain strong relationships with others, which can lead to new opportunities and collaborations.
7. Healthy eating habits: Successful people prioritize their nutrition by eating a balanced and healthy diet, which fuels their body and mind.
8. Mindfulness and self-reflection: They practice mindfulness and self-reflection regularly to stay focused on their goals, learn from their mistakes, and make adjustments when needed.

By incorporating these habits into their daily lives, successful people can maintain a healthy work-life balance, achieve their goals, and continuously grow and improve themselves.

Example of the law actually working in somones

life: There are many stories of people who have

experienced

the laws of attraction working in their lives, but one that stands out is the story of Jim Carrey, the famous actor and comedian.

As a struggling actor in the early 1980s, Jim Carrey was living in a small apartment in Los Angeles, barely making enough money to pay his bills. However, he was determined to make it big in Hollywood and fulfill his dream of becoming a successful actor.

To help him achieve his goal, Carrey started practicing the laws of attraction. He would visualize himself as a successful actor, picturing himself on the big screen and receiving standing ovations for his performances. He would also write himself a check for $10 million, dated five years in the future, and carry it around with him as a reminder of his goal.

Despite facing rejection after rejection, Carrey remained committed to his dream and kept practicing the laws of attraction. He even wrote himself a letter, pretending to be a casting director who was impressed with his acting skills and offering him a role in a big Hollywood movie.

Eventually, Carrey's hard work and positive attitude paid off. In 1994, he landed the lead role in the hit movie "Ace Ventura: Pet Detective," which catapulted him to stardom. He went on to star in many more successful movies, earning millions of dollars in the process.

Looking back on his success, Carrey credits his use of the laws of attraction for helping him achieve his goals. He says that by focusing on his dreams and visualizing himself as a successful actor, he was able to attract the opportunities and resources he needed to succeed.

Carrey's story is a powerful example of how the laws of attraction can work in someone's life, as long as they are willing to put in the hard work and stay committed to their goals.

Conclusion

We abide by the laws that our society and government have established. When these laws are strictly adhered to by every individual, the result is a more peaceful and well-organized community. The opposite is true: failure to adhere to laws or rules can result in social, environmental, or economic conflicts. Yes, laws are what govern society and allow us to coexist peacefully with others. They are also what keep us safe from harm.

The law of attraction is a universal law that applies to all situations. This universal law provides us with a clear understanding of how we should conduct ourselves in the universal society and what we should expect to receive in return. When it comes to manifesting our desires, the law of attraction states that we should not only ask for what we want but also anticipate receiving it. When we ask for something, the universe is eager to provide it for our benefit. Consider this: when a flower necessitates sunlight, the sun is made available. When a tree requires dirt to bury its roots, dirt is found for it. There is a cave available for a pregnant wolf when she is ready to give birth. Suppose any living being residing in this universe requires something to advance its own life or the universe's life as a whole. In that case, the resources are immediately made available to it. Suppose you believe that you are the only living being in the entire universe who does not deserve the resources necessary to flourish.

64

Wouldn't it be naive and perhaps even selfish of you to believe that? In my opinion, it would be impolite to do so. The universe did not create and nurture you into your current state of existence solely to deprive you of everything you require to survive. Instead, it is actively prepared to provide you with anything you may require, want, or desire to not only advance your life but also to live it to the fullest extent possible. The universal life force energy yearns to have a human experience. Because you are a living being, you are the vessel through which it gains the opportunity to experience life as a whole. Those who do not embrace and enjoy experiences perish and eventually fade away from the face of the earth. It is, quite literally, your responsibility to mobilize all of the resources that you require to live your life to the fullest extent possible, in whatever manner you see fit. When you do this, you provide the universe with the opportunity to anticipate that it will have the opportunity to experience its one true love: life!

They are completely unaware of their own ability to master the law of attraction, which they have done so without even realizing. They are preoccupied with how much their body hurts and how ill their health is, and as a result, their life is reduced to a state of constant pain and poor health. Their bodies do not appear to be the way they would like them to be, and they have a persistent sense of being in a state of chaos and destruction. They concentrate on how little money they have and how difficult it is for them to pay their bills, and as a result, less money comes in, and the struggle becomes more difficult. They are preoccupied with how little love they have in their lives or with all of how love has and continues to fail them. As a result, they are unable to attract love into their lives as they should. Because they are

66 AUSTYN INGRAM

preoccupied with how mundane, boring, or undesirable their lives are, they become even more mundane, boring, and undesirable. But here's the thing: you are the only one who fails and suffers due to your unhelpful thoughts and obsessions. No one else is affected. The universe is not in pain because it is experiencing life in one of the many forms that it can take on in its infinite variety. It seeks to understand life in all of its manifestations, and you have chosen to be the person through whom it learns to understand life in existence of suffering, pain, and death.

Amazingly, all it takes for you to make the decision to move to the other end of the spectrum is a change of heart. When you begin living your life by the opposite form of life, you will notice a significant shift in your circumstances. When you allow the universe to continue experiencing life through you in a new way, the universe will be delighted to provide you with any and all of the resources that you require to begin experiencing life in that new and exciting way. When you place your hand in the palm of the universe's hand, you have complete control over the creation of your existence. Choose where you direct your attention, where you direct your energy, and what you choose to accept and allow into your life from this point forward.

The decisions you make regarding your one-of-a-kind existence are completely up to you. The universe will always be delighted to provide you with whatever you require to continue living life through you to the fullest extent possible... The only decision you truly have to make is whether you will assist the universe in experiencing its fullest negative experiences through you or whether you will assist the universe in experiencing its fullest positive experiences through you.

As we come to the end of this journey, I ask that you please consider providing me with honest feedback on your experience with this book. I appreciate your time and consideration. We would greatly appreciate it if you could write a raving review.

Thank you, and remember how abundant you are at all times.